THE MONTESSORI BAKER

CHRISTIE ALEXANDRA DURYEA

Copyright © 2023 Christie Alexandra Duryea.

All rights reserved. No part of this book may be used or reproduced by any means, graphic, electronic, or mechanical, including photocopying, recording, taping or by any information storage retrieval system without the written permission of the author except in the case of brief quotations embodied in critical articles and reviews.

This book is a work of non-fiction. Unless otherwise noted, the author and the publisher make no explicit guarantees as to the accuracy of the information contained in this book and in some cases, names of people and places have been altered to protect their privacy.

Archway Publishing books may be ordered through booksellers or by contacting:

Archway Publishing
1663 Liberty Drive
Bloomington, IN 47403
www.archwaypublishing.com
844-669-3957

Because of the dynamic nature of the Internet, any web addresses or links contained in this book may have changed since publication and may no longer be valid. The views expressed in this work are solely those of the author and do not necessarily reflect the views of the publisher, and the publisher hereby disclaims any responsibility for them.

Any people depicted in stock imagery provided by Getty Images are models, and such images are being used for illustrative purposes only.
Certain stock imagery © Getty Images.

Interior Image Credit: Brittany Tyler Photography

ISBN: 978-1-6657-4759-2 (sc)
ISBN: 978-1-6657-4758-5 (hc)
ISBN: 978-1-6657-4760-8 (e)

Print information available on the last page.

Archway Publishing rev. date: 09/14/2023

Dedicated to Arta and Abobo

If not for these two people, my life would not be possible. I love them for everything they are and everything they made me to be.

> The hands help the development of the intellect. When a child is capable of using his hands, he can have a quantity of experiences in the environment through using them. In order to develop his consciousness, then his intellect, and then his will, he must have exercises and experiences. It is not that man must develop in order to work, but that man must work in order to develop.
> (Maria Montessori 1946, 126)

Table of Contents

Preface 1

What Is the Montessori Philosophy? 2

The Importance of Food Education 3

Food and Kitchen Safety 4

Preparing the Environment with These Tips and Techniques 13

Understanding and Presenting the Recipes 20

Recipes 23

Setting the Table and Sharing a Meal at Home 39

References 42

About the Author 43

Preface

I could not have done life without all the love in my heart for my daughter, husband, family, and friends. This book encompasses what I've learned as a chef, teacher, and mother, from observing children, the AMI training, and my entire career as a Montessori teacher. This book is for teachers, trainers, parents, and any adult who wants to bake with a child (eighteen months and up) while embracing the child's independence.

What Is the Montessori Philosophy?

The Montessori philosophy is based on Maria Montessori, who was an Italian physician and educator. She was innovative in her approach to teaching. She used the child's natural process and independence. She believed in preparing environments that would set children up for success. As each student attends class in a Montessori school, they are prepared for the next class and stage in their lives—infancy, primary level, elementary level, and adolescence. She showed children deep respect and gave them an education that prepared them for life.

Word of her exceptional skills as an educator spread across the world. Teachers began training under Maria Montessori and then through certified Montessori trainers. Eventually, it trickled down through the entire world. The Montessori philosophy is taught in over 140 countries. It encourages independence and self-confidence while promoting physical and psychological development. The AMI training program is Montessori's original teachings. It is very extensive and respected throughout the world.

The Importance of Food Education

Food has become more than the primary need to maintain health. Food is exploration—social and cultural. It brings families, friends, and strangers together. As caregivers, we want children to have a good relationship with food. We enjoy eating and trying new foods, so they should too. We just need to give them the opportunity and start them as young as possible. I've seen young children enjoy exotic fruits, strong spices, different textures, and bold flavors. My daughter eats all kinds of cuisines and truly enjoys the same food that we eat.

I saw a Montessori teacher give her toddler a bowl of mussels and watched her eat each mussel right out of the shell. Children have the capacity to enjoy different kinds of foods like adults do. Don't be discouraged if they won't try the food in the beginning. I still pretend that it doesn't hurt my feelings when my niece turns down my cooking. It doesn't stop me from continuing to expand her palate. I've also tried new foods while working with children. I did not always have a relationship with healthy food when I was a pastry chef, but I do now.

Food preparation embodies all areas of the Montessori philosophy. We participate in food preparation as we do with practical life skills. We take care of ourselves and our environment. We refine our gross motor skills through the movement of furniture, refine our fine motor skills through pouring, stirring, and spooning, and integrate grace and courtesy into our vocabulary. Through food preparation, children learn to make their food independently so that they can maintain health and nutrition throughout their lives. They use their gross motor skills to bring tables together for communal meals or moving chairs to sit at the table. Children have an opportunity to use grace and courtesy throughout a meal by politely asking for food, serving another person, or waiting to be served. This will help children adapt to their culture and develop a sense of belonging. Children will learn to care for their environment by clearing and cleaning the meal area. It is also important to use real food when educating children about food. Wooden and plastic pretend toys don't reach the child's senses in the same way that the enjoyment of preparing and eating real food does.

Food and Kitchen Safety

Kitchen Sanitation

In most teacher trainings, they teach the basic forms of proper kitchen sanitation like washing hands and using gloves and hairnets when handling food. Every state also has specific rules from the health department that they must follow. When you're at home, you follow your own basic, common cleanliness rules. I personally like to keep my nails short and polish free when preparing food and baking. I don't like the feeling of getting food underneath my fingernails, and for sanitation purposes, you don't want nail polish chips in your recipe. The Montessori philosophy believes that you should remove all distractions such as wearing loud nail polish colors when presenting a lesson and working with children because they're easily distracted. Then again, you can wear gloves if you can't stay away from those super-fun manicures.

I learned very important rules about storing and serving food in my safety and sanitation class at culinary school. The most important thing that they taught me in culinary school when learning about kitchen sanitation was FIFO—first in, first out. You can teach your child this basic and simple rule. You don't open a new container if there's another container already open. In a professional kitchen, I line the newer product behind the older product to make sure that I follow this rule. It's also important to label and date the open item so that I know the last time I used it, especially when taking something out of the original packaging and putting it in a new one. I'm a big fan of using stickers to label or relabel an existing container. You can also use dry erase markers if you want to limit waste, but it won't hold up that well in the freezer.

An important rule in any kitchen is being aware of the temperature danger zone (**41-145 degrees Fahrenheit**). Staying within the **TDZ** will help everyone stay healthy. I'll simplify it. Everything that needs to be cold should be stored under **41 degrees Fahrenheit**, and everything hot needs to be stored above **145 degrees Fahrenheit**. This speaks to the constant question we ask ourselves when working with children: "How long has that been out?"

Teachers and parents alike have snack time. We leave out some snack items and hope that they will be eaten as soon as possible, but that is not usually the case. Foodborne illnesses will start to be a risk when food is in the **TDZ** after four hours. What many don't know is that some foods don't need to be out quite as long for that to happen. So I like to keep a two-hour rule for all foods—just to be safe. You can eat it or put it back in the fridge. Please check with state regulations in your area. This will also give children a sense of time management while keeping them safe. Nothing is worse than a stomach virus. I like to keep all bread products and nut flours in the refrigerator or freezer because it keeps them fresher longer.

Kitchen Attire

I feel it's important to model proper kitchen etiquette, and this includes what to wear and how to conduct yourself in the kitchen. In all Montessori lessons—whether they are in school or at home—it's important to have your hair out of your face and pulled back, to remove any distracting jewelry from the body, and to demonstrate in simple movements what you want children to absorb. Maria Montessori believed that children ages zero to six absorb everything in their environment effortlessly.

Before I start any food preparation or baking lesson, I always make it a point to wash and dry my hands properly. On or near the baking table, there should be a child's chef hat and apron. In some Montessori classrooms, teachers wear aprons the entire day. If this is the case, I like to have a separate apron for baking, because unlike other lessons, this one can get messy. Next to the apron, I also have a chef's hat. I find it much easier for children to wear their chefs' outfits if I put mine on first. With my own set, I demonstrate the way to put the apron on and then the hat. Then the children get a turn to put their sets on. In your home kitchen, you can also wear matching chef hats and aprons to make food preparation much more fun.

Knives in the Kitchen

It is important to always use a cutting board that is secure and stable on the table before cutting. Placing a damp cloth or skid-free pad underneath the cutting board will help secure it. Always give your cutting board a wiggle to see if it's secure before using it. Also, keep the adults' knives safe by using a knife sharpener every other month or when you feel them dulling.

You need to know basic knife skills for safety, keeping the integrity of the food, and food to cook evenly and to be easy to eat. Since you're not running a fine-dining kitchen, there's only a few basic knife cuts that are important. When cutting anything that's not flat, make it stable by cutting the top and bottom off so that it can sit flat on your cutting board. Next, if you have something that has a skin on it, use a peeler. For thicker peels, use a very sharp paring knife or serrated knife. Once it's bare, cut around the seed and as close as possible. For the excess fruit on the seed, you can carefully trim it or do what I used to do as a child—enjoy eating around the seed. It's very messy, but it's oh so much fun.

Once you have the flesh of the fruit cut, you can slice or cube it, depending on the age of the child and what's easier and safer for them to chew and swallow.

There are three basic knives that a teacher or parent should have handy, which children will not use.
Small- or medium-sized chef's knife (large fruits or vegetables)
Small paring knife (small fruits or vegetables)
Small or medium serrated knife (bread, cakes, and loaves)

How to Demonstrate Knife Skills for Children

It's important to use very slow movements when demonstrating knife skills. You want to make sure that you're demonstrating a safe knife method as mentioned above, which they will be using directly after the demonstration. Hold knife with dominant hand, place it closely on top of the food, insert the point downward, and then cut through while rotating the wrist down to make a clean cut. Repeat one more time and then let the children have a turn. If you see that the children are having trouble, ask for another turn, make a couple more cuts, and return the knife. This is a process, and if you feel the activity is unsafe at any time, ask for a turn and finish the cutting yourself. Remember, the smaller the hand, the smaller the handle of the knife should be—like a cheese knife or crinkle cutter.

Mise en Place

Mise en place is the French culinary phrase that every chef lives by. You can't start anything without your mise en place which means to "put everything in its place". It's referring to the planning that happens before executing a recipe. This means your ingredients are ready to use and premeasured. All utensils and equipment necessary to complete the recipe are ready. This will also help you save time and keep things organized. Part of your mise en place is reading the recipe thoroughly, preparing your workspace and equipment, gathering ingredients by placing them in bowls, and setting out utensils. Every good chef follows this sequence, along with washing hands and cleaning as he or she goes. The term *mise en place* has a perfect place in the Montessori philosophy because it teaches us how important it is to prepare the adult and the environment so that the child can be as successful as possible. This will also ensure great success when presenting the recipes to children.

Setting Up the Baking Area in the Classroom

In the classroom, it's important to have a separate area for baking like a baking table. If your classroom is too small for a baking area, you can transform one of your worktables by placing a heavy and secure granite or stone slab on top. This makes it visibly different from the other tables in the room.

Just like all practical life activities, there needs to be a water source nearby and somewhere to wash hands before and after the activity.

You put all the pre-measured ingredients on a tray, on the table, in a row, remembering to place from left to right in order of usage. You can place the kitchen utensils on the left side of the bowl or in a container on the table. An apron and chef hat should be on the table or hanging at arm's reach. It's important to place a bin underneath or near the baking table so that children can dispose of dirty dishes. Those same children or other kids can clean those dishes at the dishwashing table or help place them in the dishwasher. There should be a timer so that the child can visibly see and hear when it's time to check the contents in the oven.

Setting Up the Baking Area at Home

There are many ways to create a baking area in your home. You can make a Montessori kitchen for your children. Transform a children's play kitchen into a functional kitchen. By putting a cutting board over the stove of the fake kitchen, your child will have a workspace. For the water source, you can replace the fake spout with a drink dispenser or install a water sprout that connects to a gallon jug underneath and inside the kitchen. Both work great, and children can use them to wash their hands before and after food activities. You can also add a small table with a stone slab and chair, which you can use as a baking table. Lastly, if you have space for a learning tower or a secure and safe step stool in your kitchen, this can be convenient for some adults who don't want to bend over or do want to food prep alongside the child. It must be in a space where you can always see the child.

Gathering Ingredients

It's important to gather the best ingredients for any recipe. When choosing your ingredients, try to shop local, fresh, organic, non-GMO, and unprocessed foods as much as possible. All of the recipes in this book can be made with ingredients that promote a healthier style of baking with children. Sugar is in all the recipes, but I stay away from any kind of refined sugars, so you'll only see natural sweeteners like honey, maple syrup, coconut sugar, and monk-fruit sweetener. You're welcome to substitute it for any sugar you would like, but I recommend baking the recipes as is.

Some recipes call for the use of unbleached or wheat flour versus bleached flour due to the harmful qualities of the bleaching process. In some of the recipes, you'll see gluten-free flour, such as almond, coconut, and oat flour so that those who have dietary restrictions can also enjoy them. I prefer using dry, fast-acting yeast when baking with young children or when pressed for time like baking in a classroom. It's much faster than fresh or regular dry-active yeast.

Storing Food

You'll need a refrigerator for all perishable items. I like to store nut flours and nuts in the refrigerator for a longer shelf life. Whenever I find myself with extra fruit or vegetables that are about to go bad, I either add them to my recipe or freeze them for a later date. It's also important to have a nearby dry storage area that has all your other ingredients. Once they are opened, I recommend any dry ingredients to be transferred to airtight containers and labeled. As a chef, I kept tape and a sharpie nearby. It's very important to keep the sharpie away from any child. I'm sure you know why. If you want to get fancy, you can buy a label maker. It will give all your ingredients a clean and polished look. Keeping proper labels on food items will ensure that there is no food wasted.

If you want to take it up a notch, you can even have a food inventory list like a real chef does. You and your child can check it daily or weekly. This will help you keep track of everything you have and want to put on your next shopping list. If your child is too young to read, you can use pictures of the food items and then simply check them off. In culinary school, the instructor would have a **COD** (chef of the day). That student oversaw the running of the kitchen, which included checking inventory lists, preparing a list for the next day, and delegating cleaning assignments. This is a great way to teach responsibility to older children.

Finding the Proper Sized Bowls, Pans, and Kitchen Utensils

When considering the Montessori method in the kitchen, we always want to use natural-made products, but glass is my favorite option for prepped ingredients because the children can see what's inside the bowl. Picking out the right bowl depends on the child's height. You always want the bowl to be shallow enough so that he or she can see inside the bowl but tall enough so that the ingredients won't spill out. Stainless steel, copper finished, or glass are the best materials for bowls. Wood is very beautiful, but it will start to wear out after several uses, and you can't run it through the dishwasher.

There are so many options for baking pans when using small recipes. Whenever baking Bundts, loaves, and cakes, six-inch pans are the perfect size for batters. Half- and quarter-sheet pans are great for breads and bars. Of course, mini cupcake pans are used universally for cupcakes, muffins, cookies, and bread rolls. I recommend a nonstick surface for easier clean up, but you can use a good oil spray and parchment paper that is cut to the shape of the pan. This ensures that the food items will come out of the pan properly.

There are many kitchen utensils for different types of baking:

    Wooden spoons for mixing doughs
    A pastry cutter for biscuits and scones
    A spatula for batters
    A coffee measuring spoon for scooping batter
    A small wooden rolling pin for rolling out dough
    Small ramekins for measuring
    Smaller pitchers for pouring ingredients
    Hands for kneading doughs
    Tongs
    Small cutting boards for food preparation
    The three basic knives that a child can use are
    Small spreading/serrated
    Crinkle cutter
    Cheese knife

If any of these knives feel too sharp or unsafe use sandpaper to dull the knife. *Always test the knife first*. Very carefully and gently run it through your hand first. Never give a young child a knife that you don't feel comfortable with him or her putting in the mouth or holding in the hand. Please use your discretion regarding the level of maturity and responsibility that the child has before giving him or her an adult knife.

Equipment

For equipment, you'll need an oven or toaster oven, which you must keep completely out of the reach of children. When baking at home, it's important to exaggerate how hot the oven is and how it can burn (Ouch!). For cooking vegetables, you can use a steamer or microwave. I know many children who love using electric griddles for pancakes, tortillas, and flatbreads. A food dehydrator is really fun for drying fruits and meats. Small Crock-Pots are great for making applesauce, jams, and other savory dishes. If used carefully, a small waffle press for making sweet and savory waffles is also a great idea. Once the child is older or has been baking for a while, you can slowly introduce mixers, larger Crock-Pots, blenders, food processors, and cooking directly on the stove.

Preparing the Environment with These Tips and Techniques

What Activities to Start With

In general, it's all about developing and refining a child's ability to concentrate for long periods of time. In the Montessori philosophy, we believe that a child's concentration is the most important thing of all. It's so important that we never interrupt a working child unless the child is about to harm himself or herself, another child, or the materials. Young children especially have very short attention spans, so we want to build up their concentration to longer periods. If you have a young child who is around two years old who has never been in the kitchen, start with small forms of food preparation. You can start with simple food prep tasks like peeling a mandarin, helping you stir, or even standing next to you and adding things to the bowl. Remember to not have any preconceived notions the first couple times. It can be great or a disaster, but it will always be fun for you and the child. As you feel more comfortable, add more complex tasks and sequences. Never forget your mise en place.

How to Incorporate Food Preparation at Home

Incorporating your child during food preparation for family dinners isn't only fun but also can alleviate stress when your child wants your attention, but you need to cook dinner. This is especially true of picky eaters. Isn't it ironic that whenever an adult is busy, that's when a child wants their attention the most? Children really love to be included in everything. They constantly absorb everything that the adult does and usually want to replicate it. Picky eaters really know how to wear you down. Including your children in dinner preparation will really help them desire to try new foods, mostly because they were part of the process, and they are interested to know how something they made tastes. It might not happen the first couple of times. Slowly incorporating things that you know they like with a couple of new ingredients can really open their palates. Sometimes just changing the shape or brand of their favorite food will also help change their palate to be a little more accepting of new flavors.

Your children can help by chopping or sorting vegetables. Have them gather spices or ingredients. They can hunt for the ingredients in the pantry or fridge and organize them for you on the counter. You can introduce new language by passing ingredients to the children to hold, smell, feel, and taste. Creating a garden with your children is a great culinary tool, and it is wonderful for practical life skills. Make sure you pick herbs, seasonal fruits, and vegetable seeds that grow well in your climate. Incorporate practical life skills using your garden. Teach children by germinating seeds, watching them grow, and maintaining them by watering them as necessary. You can use things from your garden in your recipes. The best part about baking is planning, together, all the delicious things you want to eat. Think of good quality and healthy meals for the family. Create menus that are balanced. You can post them on the fridge or a calendar as a reminder.

Menu Planning at School

Depending on the age of your children and their dietary guidelines, you may or may not be able to plan together. With younger children, I plan snacks based on their dietary guidelines. For older children, I make menu planning a lesson, including learning dietary guidelines, filling grocery lists, shopping, delegating food prep, and kitchen sanitation. Remember that this is only a snack. You don't want children filling up, getting up from the lunch table, and not eating a well-balanced lunch. A full-day schedule will need two snacks and lunch, which is usually brought in from home. If you don't have a system in the classroom for procuring ingredients, you can send out a grocery list to a one new family each week. That's the system I've always used. I try not to pick more than eight-to-ten items every week. Some schools will also allocate weekly food budgets for their teachers so that they can shop. Larger schools that have a commercial kitchen receive a continuous shipment of food. Regardless of how you get the ingredients for your classroom, always remind parents and the administration that they should offer all children fresh, seasonal, locally sourced, organic, and minimally processed foods.

Once your menus are complete, place them where parents can see them so that they know what their children are eating. The children might be discovering different flavors, and you want your parents informed so that they can try it at home. As the food is delivered, it's important that the children are part of the proper process of storing food. We want the child to see the adult using and continually cleaning areas to prepare for the storage of new ingredients, the FIFO rule, the adult making sure that the fridge has the correct temperature to avoid falling into the TDZ, and everything being organized and labeled.

Tips for the Kitchen

Oiling Pans

I'm not a big fan of oil sprays. Although they're very quick and easy, they don't teach the child anything, and when you inhale them, they're awful. You can set out a tray with the baking pans, a small brush with natural bristles, and a small dish with your choice of oil. I always recommend natural oils like olive, coconut, or grapeseed and of course, melted butter for taste. It's best to oil the baking pan instead of using one-time-use paper or foil products. It's ecofriendly and cost effective, especially when you're baking for twelve-to-thirty children daily. It's important to note that once you've sprayed the pan and added the batter, you need to bake it right away. Sometimes the batter will sit too long, and the oil will become incorporated in the batter, causing the batter to stick during the baking process.

Working with Yeast and Proofing Dough

It's important that the liquid you're pouring yeast into is not too hot because it can damage the yeast. If it's too cold, it will take longer to proof. Warm water of **105–115** degrees Fahrenheit is optimal, but warm to the touch will do. To avoid clumping, sprinkle yeast. This means slowly adding and thoroughly spreading it around the bowl to the top of the water. You'll know your yeast is fully incorporated because the water will be cloudy, and there will be no clumps.

It's extremely important to grease any bowl or pan you use for proof. The oil will allow the dough to rise and proof properly. Humidity is also important, so if you don't have a proofer setting on your oven or a humid place to proof your dough, you can cover the dough with a warm damp cloth. Also, proofing times vary depending on climate. For instance, I live in Florida where it's usually hot and humid. Even indoors, any dough will proof much quicker than in cold, dry places, which will need extra heat, humidity, and time. The reason why most of my recipes say "proof until it's doubled in size" is because it varies depending on your climate. Yeast is very temperamental, so never directly add salt to it because it will kill it.

Rolling Doughs

Parchment paper and wax paper are the best way to roll dough without having a sticky mess or an excess of flour. It's important to know beforehand, how wide you're rolling your dough because you want the parchment paper to be the size of the final product. This will help the child gage when to stop. You will cut two identical pieces in a round or square shape. If you want round dough or cookies, you should start with a rounded piece of dough. The same concept is applied to a square. A square might be a more challenging shape to roll, but it does attribute for less waste. It is great when you're rolling biscuits or crackers.

Lay one piece on the table, lightly flour the parchment paper, place the dough in the middle of the parchment paper, flour the top, and place the second piece of parchment on top. With the palm of your hand, press the parchment paper into the dough, and it's ready for rolling. The child can roll the dough until it reaches the edges of the parchment paper. Depending on the recipe, place it in the refrigerator for a couple minutes or overnight. When you're ready to work with the dough again, simply remove one of the parchment sheets. You can use any cutter directly on the parchment paper and bake directly after. I love this technique because it's easy to clean up, and we're setting the child up for success. You can also reuse the same parchment sheet for baking.

Kneading Doughs

It's important to knead dough on a lightly floured surface. As you're mixing the dough in the bowl, you want it to come together as much as possible before kneading it with your hands on a surface. If the dough is too sticky, sprinkle more flour onto your kneading surface and your hands. It's important to remember that whatever flour you add to your surface will be incorporated into your dough, so sprinkle lightly, knead until the dough is smooth, and don't overwork the dough. You'll know that your dough has been overworked if it's too tight. If the dough is too hard, you've added too much flour. You can try to incorporate some water avoid the dough becoming too firm. As you're kneading the dough, tuck the dough into a ball. Move it in circular motions and use the palms of your hands as they brush against the surface. The perfect dough will be in the shape of a ball, smooth, not too sticky, and easy to transfer onto to a sheet pan or into a greased bowl for proofing.

Cross Utilization

Cross utilization is the method of using a certain ingredient in different recipes. In professional kitchens, cross utilization is important for efficiency and keeping food costs down. When working with children, I also use it as a food-cost tool because every week in my classroom, a grocery list goes to one family. It's important for me that the list is kept to a minimum, to be considerate of the family's budget.

At home, the same idea is kept. You know that you're going to use flour, eggs, sugar, butter, oil, and leavening agents in baking projects. If you're making a certain recipe and it calls for a fruit that you don't have, see if you have something that you can substitute for it. You can get a couple ingredients that you can cross utilize. For example, if you have blueberries, you can serve them on their own, make muffins, scones, or fruit salad, freeze them, and use them later. In a Montessori environment, you can cross utilize anything from food preparation to baking. For example, if you have apples, you can slice some of them. Then you can use some of those apples for baking or even make applesauce. The possibilities are endless. It can be a fun game to play with children when you ask them, "How many different things can we make with a tomato?" Then they must think of all the wonderful things that they can make with just one ingredient.

Placing the Mixture into a Baking Dish

If baking bread, have the child use a small brush and some cooking oil to grease the sheet pan or line the sheet pan with parchment paper. Model how to transfer the dough onto a sheet pan. If baking batter, you can have the child grease the pan with a small brush and cooking oil as well. Then use a small scoop or tablespoon to scoop batter into a baking dish. Always use a spatula to remove excess batter from bowl.

Placing a Dish in the Oven

Depending on the child's skill, you or the child can safely walk the baking dish to the oven. You will place it in, modeling with two hands. Then always emphasizing how *hot* the oven is. Show and discuss how long the timer is set for.

During the Baking Process, Clean Up

The child can take the tray or tub to the sink and wash the dishes. If you have a dishwasher, you can model how to place each container in the dishwasher. Place your apron in the laundry basket. Finish each baking tutorial or food preparation time by washing hands.

Time's Up!

As soon as you hear your timer go off, make sure to alert the child. Together you can walk to the oven and check out your treat. It may or may not need more time. If it's ready, make sure to model putting on oven-safe gloves and using two hands while slowly removing it from the oven and placing it away from the child to cool off. Once the treat is cool, portion or pop it out for eating. Enjoy it.

Understanding and Presenting the Recipes

Understanding the Recipes

Read the recipes in this book thoroughly, pay careful attention to its tips and techniques, and test the recipes. It will give extra details for understanding each recipe thoroughly. Some of the tips and techniques will not relate to each recipe while some will be interchangeable. My pro tips are a great addition to my recipes. They give creative ideas to an already existing recipe. If you're feeling brave, just go for it!

Presenting the Recipes

The age of the child will tell you how to approach each presentation. Each recipe will have a general sequence of directions, which tell the way that an adult would make it. We will break down these tips when presenting them to a child. If you're presenting them for the first time to a child, you need to plan, buy ingredients, test the recipes, and have the mise en place before the child comes into the environment. Activities that are done in the environment or at home must be prepared in advance, unless you have a child who is experienced enough to help in the process or do it independently. At home, you can plan by picking a recipe, going shopping, and setting it up together.

You can make recipe cards for older children. If the child doesn't know how to read, you can place pictures of ingredients and actions on the card. As we're setting up the mise en place for each recipe, it's very important that we put each ingredient in a different container. Not only are we teaching the child the process of baking but also teaching language. It's better for the child to clearly see the ingredients when describing them. Each ingredient should be set up and presented from left to right in the order that it will be used. The Montessori philosophy in the US believes that this is the progression of the way children's hands work because they learn to read and write from left to right. Use both hands when reaching for something, mixing, or pouring, unless it involves minimal effort. You always want to have one hand holding the bowl and the other hand using the kitchen utensil. Remember, you are much stronger than children are. You need to model what you want them to do. When you present a recipe, describe the action and then demonstrate it. Young children have difficulty dividing their attention. Young children need time to listen or complete a task.

Use slow movements when demonstrating anything. If you feel like the child missed a part of your demonstration or that the child isn't modeling the movements well, next time you present the same food preparation, you emphasize the movements that you believe the child missed or needs further instruction and practice on. Make sure to use your dominant hand for mixing and your other hand for holding the side of the bowl so that it remains steady. You want the child to be as independent as possible, but if the mixture isn't completely mixed, you can simply ask for a turn and continue to model mixing. You can say, "I still see flour on the side of the bowl. I'm going to mix it in. Watch." It's always a good idea for the adult to give it one last mix to make sure ingredients are evenly incorporated. Since each ingredient is measured and placed in its own container, it's crucial that you add one ingredient at a time, demonstrating how to pour and mix it and then giving the child a turn to do so. It's also important to name the ingredient each time. "Now I'm going to pour the oil in. Watch." Demonstrate pouring it in. "Now I'm going to mix it in, Watch." Demonstrate mixing. "Would you like a turn?" You give the child an opportunity to pour each ingredient and mix in between.

Recipes

Coconut Loaf

Yields **3** mini loaves

Ingredients

6 whole eggs
1 teaspoon vanilla
½ cup coconut oil
1 cup coconut sugar
⅔ cup coconut flour
2 teaspoons baking powder
½ teaspoon salt
3 tablespoons shredded coconut (set aside)

Preparation

Preheat the oven to **350** degrees Fahrenheit. Grease three mini-loaf pans and set aside.

In a medium-size bowl, mix eggs, vanilla, coconut oil, and sugar with a wooden spoon or spatula until incorporated. Add coconut flour, baking powder, and salt and mix until fully incorporated.

Use coffee scoop or spoon to add mixture to loaf pans. Sprinkle coconut flakes evenly on top of each loaf.

Bake loaves for **10–15** minutes. Check with a toothpick after the first ten minutes and give it more time if needed.

Storage

You can individually wrap loaves with plastic wrap and store in the fridge for up to four days. You can also slice and reheat in the oven at **350** degrees Fahrenheit for **5–10** minutes or until warm.

Pro Tip

You can also bake these in any size muffin tins. Depending on pan size, baking time will be different. When the loaves are done, the coconut flakes on top will be a perfect golden brown. You can add ½ cup of chopped pineapple to make it piña colada flavored. You can also enjoy with butter or fresh whipped cream.

Strawberry Basil Donuts with Lemon Glaze

Yields **6** donuts

Ingredients

Strawberry Basil Donuts

1 whole egg
½ cup monkfruit sweetener
½ stick melted butter
½ teaspoon vanilla extract
¼ cup milk
¼ cup yogurt
¾ cup non-bleached, all-purpose flour
¼ teaspoon baking powder
⅛ teaspoon salt
¼ cup mashed strawberries
2 teaspoons basil

Lemon Glaze

1 cup Swerve confectioner's sugar
1 tablespoon lemon juice

Preparation

Donuts

Preheat Oven to **350** degrees Fahrenheit. Grease a six-size donut pan and set aside.

In a medium-size bowl, mix egg and monkfruit sweetener together and then whisk until incorporated. Add melted butter, vanilla, milk, and yogurt and whisk together. Fold in flour, baking powder, and salt until incorporated. Add mashed strawberries and basil and fold in until fully incorporated.

Spoon batter evenly into donut pan. Bake for **10** minutes and then check with a toothpick. Add more time if needed. After donuts come out of the oven, remove from pans, let cool, and start the glaze recipe.

Glaze

In a small bowl, place Swerve confectioner's sugar and lemon juice and whisk until smooth. You can add more lemon juice if too thick. You can dunk donuts in or drizzle the glaze. Dust with Swerve or eat plain.

Storage

These donuts are best eaten fresh. You can store them in an airtight container in the fridge for up to two days.

Pro Tip

Garnish with strawberries, chopped basil, and lemon zest for a natural decoration. Add your choice of sprinkles for a fun decoration.

Orange Blackberry Honey Muffins

Yields 24 mini muffins

Ingredients

½ whole egg
6 tablespoons honey
3 tablespoons grapeseed oil
3 tablespoons milk
¾ cup non-bleached, all-purpose flour
1 teaspoon baking powder
⅛ teaspoon salt
¼ cup lightly chopped blackberries
2 teaspoons small orange zest

Preparation

Preheat oven to 350 degrees Fahrenheit. Grease or line two mini cupcake pans and set aside.

In a medium-size bowl, whisk egg, honey, grapeseed oil, and milk until incorporated. Add flour, baking powder, salt and whisk until fully incorporated. Fold in blackberries and orange zest until all ingredients are incorporated.

Use coffee scoop or small spoon to add mixture to muffin pans. Bake for 10 minutes and then check with a toothpick. Add more time if needed.

Storage

After muffins are completely cool, you can place them in an airtight bag or container and keep for up to five days in the fridge.

Pro Tip

Garnish with your choice of chopped nuts. The base of the muffin mixture is very versatile, as you can add any kind of flavor combinations, such as fruits, dried fruit, chocolate chips, different zests, and even herbs, by just substituting them for the blackberries and orange zest.

Fresh Herbed Focaccia

Yields a quarter-sheet pan

Ingredients

1 ½ cups warm water
2 tablespoons dry active yeast
2 tablespoons honey
1 cup bread flour
½ cup whole-wheat flour
2 tablespoons Italian herbs
2 teaspoons garlic
2 teaspoons salt

Preparation

Preheat the oven to **375** degrees Fahrenheit. Grease and line a quarter-sheet pan. Set aside.

In a medium-size bowl, add warm water and then sprinkle in yeast. Whisk until the water is cloudy and there are no clumps of yeast or pieces on the sides of the bowl. Whisk honey into mixture until combined. Add bread and whole-wheat flours, herbs, and garlic. Mix until somewhat combined and then add salt. Combine until it makes a ball.

Sprinkle flour on the table and dump dough right on top. Knead until dough is slightly sticky. If too sticky, add some flour to hands and/or dough and continue to knead. Place ball of dough onto sheet pan. Softly massage and spread dough with fingertips to the corners of the sheet pan. Proof for fifteen minutes or until it's doubled in size. You can add more finger indentations in your dough before the oven or leave as is for a smoother finish.

Bake for **10–15** minutes or until golden brown. Let cool and cut into cubes.

Storage

After bread has completely cooled, you can wrap large pieces in plastic wrap and place in fridge for up to five days. If pieces are already cut small, you can place in fridge for up to two days. Place in oven at **350** degrees Fahrenheit for **5–10** minutes and then serve.

Pro Tip

Try to use fresh herbs and garlic. Make deep indentations for the focaccia look. Right after the bread comes out of the oven, brush or drizzle with olive oil and sprinkle crunchy salt like Maldon. You can also serve with a side of marinara, balsamic vinegar, butter, or tapenade. You can also use the bread to make sandwiches or my personal favorite, pizza.

Mangoes and Cream Bundt

Yields **1** (6-inch) Bundt pan

Ingredients

- **1** whole egg
- ½ cup honey
- ¼ cup yogurt
- **1** cup flour
- ¼ teaspoon baking soda
- ⅛ teaspoon salt
- ½ stick butter, melted
- ½ cup chopped mangoes

Preparation

Preheat the oven to **350** degrees Fahrenheit. Grease Bundt pan and set aside.

In a medium-size mixing bowl, add egg, honey, and yogurt and whisk until incorporated. Add flour, baking soda, and salt and mix until incorporated. Fold in melted butter. Add chopped mangoes and mix until fully incorporated.

Pour batter into Bundt pan and place in the oven. Bake for **15–20** minutes or until toothpick comes out clean.

Storage

After the Bundt has completely cooled, you can place in an airtight container and keep for up to three days in the fridge.

Pro Tip

There are so many different fruits that you can replace mangoes with, but I recommend seasonal and local fruit. Some great fruit ideas are peaches, berries, apples, papayas, and pineapples. To garnish, dust with powdered sugar or Swerve confectioner's sugar.

Pizza Rolls

Yields 24 mini pizza rolls

Ingredients

Dough

1 cup warm water
1 packet dry active yeast
1 tablespoon honey
2 cups unbleached, all-purpose flour
1 teaspoon salt

Pizza Rolls

1 cup pizza sauce
2 cups grated mozzarella

Preparation

Dough

Preheat the oven to 350 degrees Fahrenheit. Grease two mini cupcake pans and set aside.

In a medium-size bowl, pour water, sprinkle yeast, and whisk until yeast has dissolved. Add honey and mix until incorporated. Slightly fold in flour and then add salt. Mix with spatula or by hand until dough forms into a ball.

Place dough on floured surface and knead until smooth. Cut or tear dough into twenty-four pieces and place on greased pans.

Pizza Roll Assembly

Once the dough has been placed into pans, spoon a small amount of pizza sauce on top of each piece of dough. Then evenly sprinkle mozzarella cheese on each piece of dough.

Bake for 10-15 minutes or until cheese is golden brown.

Storage

After the pizza rolls have completely cooled, you can store them in an airtight, plastic bag or container in the fridge for up to three days. Make sure to reheat at **350** degrees Fahrenheit for **5–10** minutes before serving.

Pro Tip

Try not to get any cheese on the pan because it causes cheese to burn and stick. You can add chopped pepperoni, Italian sausage, vegetables, or any other fun pizza topping.

White-Chocolate Almond-Nut Cookies

Yields 1 dozen (2-ounce) cookies

Ingredients

1 egg white
¼ cup monkfruit sweetener
½ stick butter, melted
1 ½ cups almond flour
½ teaspoon salt
¼ cup white-chocolate chips

Preparation

Preheat the oven to 350 degrees Fahrenheit. Line sheet tray with parchment paper and set aside.

In a medium-size bowl, add egg white and monkfruit sweetener. Mix with spatula until incorporated. Mix in melted butter until combined. Add almond flour, salt, and white-chocolate chips and stir until fully incorporated.

Use coffee scooper to scoop cookie dough onto to sheet pan. Bake for 8–12 minutes or until golden on top.

Let cool. Eat plain, drizzle with white chocolate, or add chopped, toasted almonds.

Storage

After cookies have completely cooled down, you can store them in an airtight bag or container at room temperature for up to four days.

Pro Tip

You can use Lily's white-chocolate chips for less sugar. You can also add any kind of nuts or chocolate chips that you prefer. You can use a 2-ounce metal scoop to make perfectly shaped cookies or even ball them in your hand and place on sheet tray. For a chewy cookie, bake for less time. For a crunchier cookie, bake longer. You can also pat each piece of cookie dough down for a wider cookie or leave rounded for a chewy and crunchy texture.

Mini Chocolate Raspberry Cakes (Gluten Free)

Yields **12** mini cakes

Ingredients

- ¼ cup semisweet chocolate pieces, melted
- ½ stick butter, melted
- 2 eggs
- 2 tablespoons monkfruit sweetener
- ¼ cup cocoa powder
- ¼ teaspoon baking powder
- 12 raspberries

Preparation

Preheat the oven to **350** degrees Fahrenheit. Grease one mini cupcake pan and set aside.

In a medium-size bowl, add melted chocolate and butter. Gently whisk until combined. Add eggs and gently mix. Add monkfruit sweetener and mix until incorporated. Fold in cocoa powder and baking powder until fully incorporated.

Use coffee scooper to drop batter into mini cupcake pan. Make sure cups are filled evenly. Place one raspberry with its top side up and in the middle of the batter of each cake. Bake **8–10** minutes or until sides of the cake have started to rise.

Storage

After the mini cakes have completely cooled, you can store them in an airtight bag or container in the fridge for up to three days.

Pro Tip

Use Lily's chocolate chips for less sugar. Bake less time for a gooey cake. Enjoy this cake with whipped cream or ice cream.

Cinnamon-Scented Almond and Banana Chips

Yields about 1 ½ cups

Ingredients

1 tablespoon butter, melted
1 tablespoon maple syrup
¼ teaspoon cinnamon
¼ teaspoon salt
1 cup banana chips
½ cup almonds

Preparation

Preheat the oven to **350** degrees Fahrenheit. Line a sheet pan with parchment paper and set aside.

In a medium-size mixing bowl, add melted butter, maple syrup, cinnamon, and salt. Mix with a spatula until fully incorporated. Add banana chips and almonds. Fold into mixture until banana chips and almonds are evenly coated.

Pour onto the sheet pan and place in the oven. Bake for **10-12** minutes or until golden brown.

Let cool and enjoy.

Storage

After the chips have completely cooled, you can store them in an airtight bag or container at room temperature for up to five days.

Pro Tip

This is such a great on-the-go snack. Store in an airtight container to maintain freshness. You can also use your preference of nuts.

Maple Bacon Corn Bread

Yields a **9x9** baking dish

Ingredients

2 eggs
½ cup maple syrup
4 ounces butter, melted
1 cup unbleached, all-purpose flour
1 cup yellow cornmeal
3 teaspoons baking powder
1 teaspoon salt
1 cup milk
4 strips of bacon, chopped

Preparation

Preheat the oven to **350** degrees Fahrenheit. Grease and line baking dish and then set aside.

In a medium-size bowl, add eggs and maple syrup. Whisk until incorporated. Add butter and mix until incorporated. Add in flour, cornmeal, baking powder, and salt. Mix until incorporated. Pour in milk and mix until incorporated. Add bacon and mix until fully incorporated.

Pour mixture into baking dish. Bake for **12–15** minutes or until toothpick comes out clean. Let cool, cut into squares, and enjoy.

Storage

After corn bread has completely cooled down, you can store it in an airtight bag or container in the fridge for up to three days.

Pro Tip

Drizzle with honey and top with chopped bacon for extra flavor. You can also add shredded cheese, chives, or other herbs. I personally like to add honey, salt, and bacon to butter for a side of honey bacon butter for the corn bread.

A Lot of Stuff Granola

Yields about 2 cups

Ingredients

2 tablespoons coconut oil, melted
¼ cup maple syrup
¼ teaspoon salt
1 cup rolled oats
½ cup plain cornflakes
½ cup assorted nuts
½ cup assorted dried fruits

Preparation

Preheat oven to 350 degrees Fahrenheit. Line a sheet pan with parchment paper and set aside.

In a medium-size bowl, add melted coconut oil, maple syrup, and salt. Mix with a spatula until fully incorporated. Add all other ingredients. Mix until fully incorporated and everything is coated evenly.

Pour onto sheet pan. With the spatula, evenly spread mixture. Place in the oven. Bake for 15–20 minutes or until golden brown.

Storage

After granola has completely cooled, you can store it in an airtight bag or container at room temperature for up to five days.

Pro Tip

This recipe is very versatile, in the sense that you can really substitute anything you prefer. You can add 1 cup of your favorite trail mix instead of the assorted nuts and dried fruit.

Homemade Cilantro Ranch

Yields **10**-ounce bottle

Ingredients

½ cup buttermilk
½ cup mayonnaise
½ cup sour cream
2 teaspoons fresh chopped parsley
2 teaspoons fresh chopped cilantro
1 teaspoon onion powder
1 teaspoon garlic powder
1teaspoon lime juice
½ teaspoon salt

Preparation

Set aside a **12**-ounce bottle with airtight lid and a small funnel.
In a medium-size mixing bowl, add all ingredients and whisk until fully incorporated.
Place funnel inside the bottle and use small scoop to pour mixture into bottle.

Storage

Enjoy right away or label, date, and store in refrigerator for up to a week.

Pro Tip

I like to add some lime zest for extra flavor. If you don't enjoy the flavor of cilantro, you can substitute with fresh dill. This ranch goes well with different types of veggies and snacks.

Setting the Table and Sharing a Meal at Home

Setting the Table

If you're having a children's table, your children don't quite know how to set a table, and you want to teach them how to be more independent, you can make or purchase Montessori tablecloths or place mats. A Montessori tablecloth or place mat is child sized, and it has an embroidered outline of a glass, plate, and silverware. They're easy to make, and every AMI toddler Montessori teacher has made one for their training and has continued making them for their classrooms.

If you're making a tablecloth for the children's table, measure the table, which is usually the size of a large cloth dinner napkin. Make sure to prewash everything because the fabric shrinks. Lay it on a flat surface. With a fabric pen or pencil, trace the outline of a cup, plate, fork, and spoon. I find it best if you flip over the plate and glass, making wider circles, so that the plate and glass fit well on the cloth. After you've outlined the cloth and have a pattern, it's time to start embroidering by hand or with a sewing machine. If you're embroidering by hand, you'll need embroidery floss, needles, and a hoop. Put your fabric on the hoop and embroider away! Once you've embroidered your cloth, you can attach it two ways: sow two strings to each corner so that you can tie them to each of the table legs or sew an elastic band on each corner so that you can stretch it over each corner of the tabletop and secure it in place. This method is great for small children who are constantly moving the tablecloth.

If you want to make place mats so that your children can eat independently or with the family, cut a regular place mat in half—preferably one of a set so that they can all look uniform on the table together. Fold over and sew the edge you've cut. Then use the same method of embroidery. For older children, you can just use normal-size tablecloths and place mats.

Serving

In a Montessori classroom, children learn to serve themselves and others. Communal meals offer social experiences. They also offer the ability to practice grace, courtesy, manners, and etiquette, collaborate with others, develop movement, acquire a sense of belonging, care for themselves, adapt to their culture, integrate their will, and advance their independence.

When having a communal meal at home, the table should be set for everyone who is participating in the meal. To keep a child seated, everyone should stay seated throughout the meal. One person can assist in the process. Depending on the meal, I recommend serving items family style, as we do in the classroom. This takes the stress off the children during the meal because they get to choose what goes on their plates. The adults should serve themselves the first item and then pass it around the table so that the children can model their movements. It's important to use language throughout the meal. You can say, "Look, green beans. I'm going to put some on my plate. Watch." Model putting a few green beans on your plate and pass the bowl.

You can use a collection of different-size bowls. You don't have to put everything that you cooked in these bowls, as the bowls can get heavy. You want children to realize that they can always get more throughout the meal. Adult-size spoons are a good size. Small gravy ladles are good for serving soft foods. Set out a small water pitcher for the children so that they can practice pouring their own water. It's also very important that you acknowledge the children and the food that they have prepared.

Table Rules

Children need to be seated during the meal. You can say, "Food is for the children that are seated." If a child continues to get up from the table or throws food, you can remove the food and offer it at a later time. If the child dislikes the food, you can take it off the plate. The important rule is that they finish what's on their plates to get more, unless they tried and didn't like it. The adult must always sit with the child and model staying seated. It's important for children to see you seated, because if they don't, they will get up. Conversation is part of the experience. This is a good time to do language activities, such as self-expression and the questioning game. Take your time, do not rush, and enjoy. Children are learning and developing self-esteem. They can see the results of their actions. They can see everyone enjoying what they made. This will help them adapt and build confidence. This is also a great time to model grace and courtesy. You can model proper table manners, saying please and thank you when serving and eating together.

Cleaning Up

Make sure that you have everything you need to clean the food area. You will need a compost or trash can that is easily accessible for children. It's optional to have a spatula or small scraper so that they can clean the food from their plates. You can have your children put them directly into the dishwasher, sink, or a small cart that you use for dirty dishes. The dish cart is organized by separate compartments for cups/glasses, plates, silverware, place mats, and napkins. You can use a small three-compartment rolling cart. Once the children have put away their plates, utensils, and cups, you can continue to clear the table. If using a place mat, the children can shake their place mats of extra food in the trash and place them in the laundry. You can have a small dustpan nearby so that the children can clean up crumbs or anything on the floor from the meal. Once the meal area is clean, they can go to the bathroom to wash their hands and faces. Have them use wet cloths. All these tasks are great for developing and refining fine and gross motor skills, which will help them advance toward independence.

References

Montessori, Maria. London Lectures.

About the Author

I was born and raised in Miami, Florida. My family members were immigrants from Cuba, and this Cuban heritage started my passion for food and exploring different cultures. My parents loved to travel, which built my interest in traveling and trying new cuisines. My grandmother cooked traditional Cuban food for my family, along with the occasional spaghetti dinner and takeout. It wasn't until high school that I widened my tastes and found my interest in baking. After high school, I attended Johnson and Wales University, where I got my degree in baking and pastry arts.

I worked as a professional pastry chef for eleven years. During that time, I met my husband, Matthew, who was the chef de cuisine in a nearby restaurant. While in Miami, we fell in love and decided to move to central Florida. We had both had a change of heart. We wanted to eventually start a family and knew that working all those hours in a kitchen would make family time difficult. Matthew went into law enforcement, and shortly afterward, I discovered the Montessori philosophy.

I first worked in administration for a small Montessori school. Not long after that when I was needed, I became the substitute teacher for their toddler, primary, and elementary programs. The toddler program stole my heart. I found it to be such a wonderful age, and I especially loved that we baked every day. I then knew I wanted to become a **0-3** Montessori teacher. It was through the AMI training program in the Montessori Institute of Atlanta that I became certified as a **0-3** assistant to infancy and found my true cosmic task. I went from training to a well-known and respected Montessori school in the town where I lived and became the lead guide to one of the toddler programs.

I want to add a special acknowledgement to my beautiful, wonderful, and intelligent niece. You inspire me every day. Titi loves you!

Don't forget to follow @MontessoriTeachBake for more pictures, videos, recipes, tips, and techniques.

Check out my Etsy shop for baking inspired attire at www.etsy.com/shop/MontessoriTeachBake.